WORKBOOK

Companion For

Girl, Wash Your Face

Stop Believing the Lies About Who You Are So You Can Become Who You Were Meant To Be

By Rachel Hollis

BJ Richards

Notification:

This is a workbook and is based on and meant to accompany the original work by Rachel Hollis, *Girl, Wash Your Face: Stop Believing the Lies About Who You Are So You Can Become Who You Were Meant To Be*. It is not meant to replace the original work. If you have not read the original work, it is highly recommended you purchase it in conjunction with or prior to using this summary.

This is a workbook and is meant for educational and entertainment purposes only and has not been authorized, approved, licensed or endorsed by the original book's author or publisher and any of their licensees or affiliates.

All references in this summary to "Ms. Hollis" or "Ms. Hollis'" are referring to Rachel Hollis, author of *Girl, Wash Your Face: Stop Believing the Lies About Who You Are So You Can Become Who You Were Meant To Be*.

All references in this summary to "Ms. Hollis' original work" are referring to Rachel Hollis, author of *Girl, Wash Your Face: Stop Believing the Lies About Who You Are So You Can Become Who You Were Meant To Be*.

Copyright and Disclaimer

Copyright © 2019, BJ Richards

All rights reserved. No part of this publication may be reproduced, distributed, or transmitted in any form or by any means, including photocopying, scanning, recording, or other electronic or mechanical methods, without the prior written permission of BJ Richards, except in the case of brief quotations embodied in critical reviews and certain other noncommercial uses permitted by copyright law.

Distribution of this book without the prior permission of BJ Richards is illegal, and therefore punishable by law. It is not legal to reproduce, duplicate or transmit any part of this document either in printed format or electronically. It is strictly prohibited to record this publication and storage of the document is not allowed without written permission from the BJ Richards. All rights reserved.

Disclaimer:

Legal Notice: - BJ Richards and the accompanying materials have used their best efforts in preparing the material. This book has been composed with the best intention of providing correct and reliable information. The information provided is offered solely for informational purposes and is universal as so. This information is presented without contract or any type of guarantee assurance.

This is an unofficial summary/analysis/review meant for educational and entertainment purposes only and has not been authorized, approved, licensed or endorsed by the original book's author or publisher and any of their licensees or affiliates.

BJ Richards makes no representation or warranties with respect to the accuracy, applicability, fitness or completeness of the contents of this book. The information contained in this book is strictly for educational purposes and entertainment purposes only. Therefore, if you wish to apply ideas contained in this book, you are taking full responsibility for your actions.

BJ Richards disclaims any warranties (express or implied), merchantability, or fitness for any particular purpose. BJ Richards shall in no event be held liable to any party for any direct, indirect, punitive, special, incidental or other consequential damages arising directly or indirectly from any use of this material, which is provided "as is", and without warranties.

Any and all trademarks, product names, logos, brands and other trademarks featured or referred to within this publication are owned by their respective trademark publications and owners themselves, are not affiliated with this book and are for clarifying purposes only.

BJ Richards does not warrant the performance, effectiveness or applicability of any sites listed or linked to in this book. All links are for information purposes only and are not warranted for content, accuracy or any other implied or explicit purpose.

Recommended Books

Girl, Wash Your Face: Stop Believing the Lies About Who You Are So You Can Become Who You Were Meant To Be by Rachel Hollis. You can find it here: https://www.amazon.com/Girl-Wash-Your-Face-Believing-ebook/dp/B072TMB75T

You may also be interested in some of my other books:

1) Find out what coconut oil can really do for you without all the hype. Check out my best-selling book: *Coconut Oil Breakthrough: Boost Your Brain, Burn the Fat, Build Your Hair* by BJ Richards

Check it out here: https://www.amazon.com/Coconut-Oil-Breakthrough-Boost-Brain-ebook/dp/B01EGBA1FW/

2) Do you have a dog? Here's another best seller you may be interested in. You'll find out to deal with a number of issues safely and inexpensively at home. Find out all about it in my best-seller: *Coconut Oil and My Dog: Natural Pet Health for My Canine Friend* by BJ Richards

You can check it out here: https://www.amazon.com/Coconut-Oil-My-Dog-Natural-ebook/dp/B01MUF93U1/

3) Did you know apple cider vinegar and baking soda have some amazing health benefits? Plus, you can use them for so many things in the home and save a ton of money.

You'll find out all about it my boxset: *Apple Cider Vinegar and Baking Soda 101 for Beginners Box Set* by BJ Richards

Check it out here: https://www.amazon.com/Apple-Cider-Vinegar-Baking-Beginners-ebook/dp/B07DPCLWGB/

You can also go my website to find even more books I've written and some recommended by other authors: https://bjrichardsauthor.com

Table Of Contents

Notification 2

Copyright and Disclaimer 3

Recommended Books 4

How To Use This Workbook for Greater Personal Growth 8

Background Story of Rachel Hollis 10

Introduction: Hey Girl, Hey! 11

Chapter One 15

The Lie: Something Else Will Make Me Happy 15

Chapter Two 19

The Lie: I'll Start Tomorrow 19

Chapter Three 23

The Lie: I'm Not Good Enough 23

Chapter Four 27

The Lie: I'm Better Than You 27

Chapter Five 31

The Lie: Loving Him Is Enough For Me 31

Chapter Six 35

The Lie: No Is The Final Answer 35

Chapter Seven: 40

The Lie: I'm Bad At Sex 40

Chapter Eight 44

The Lie: I Don't Know How To Be A Mom 44

Chapter Nine 48

The Lie: I'm Not A Good Mom 48

Chapter Ten 52

The Lie: I Should Be Further Along By Now 52

Chapter Eleven 56

The Lie: Other People's Kids Are So Much Cleaner/Better Organized/More Polite 56

Chapter 12	61
The Lie: I Need To Make Myself Smaller	61
Chapter 13	65
The Lie: I'm Going To Marry Matt Damon	65
Chapter Fourteen	69
The Lie: I'm A Terrible Writer	69
Chapter Fifteen:	73
I Will Never Get Past This	73
Chapter Sixteen	77
The Lie: I Can't Tell The Truth	77
Chapter Seventeen	80
The Lie: I Am Defined By My Weight	80
Chapter Eighteen	84
The Lie: I Need A Drink	84
Chapter Nineteen	88
The Lie: There's Only One Right Way To Be	88
Chapter Twenty	92
The Lie: I Need A Hero	92
Thank you	95
Recommended Reading	96
You may also be interested in some of my other books	96

How To Use This Workbook for Greater Personal Growth

If you're beginner, that's great! My main goal for writing this workbook was so a complete newbie can start to get immediate help in implementing the lessons Ms. Hollis has presented in her book: *Girl, Wash Your Face: Stop Believing the Lies About Who You Are so You Can Become Who You Were Meant To Be*.

This workbook is as a companion guide to Ms. Hollis' original work and is not meant to replace it. I do recommend you purchase the original work by Rachel Hollis to get the most benefit from this workbook.

You'll find that the chapters are broken down into the following three parts to make it easier for you to implement the steps mentioned is Ms. Hollis' original work. Those parts are:

- Key Points
- Summary / Analysis
- Questions and/or Exercises

Key Points: Here I will outline key points I believe were most important in relaying the powerful message presented by Ms. Hollis in the original work.

Summary / Analysis: This is my summarization and analysis of the written content of the chapter.

Questions/Exercises: These are set up to help you personalize and implement the material found in Ms. Hollis' original work. This is done in such a way that you can use these steps and exercises to further develop a clear road map of your own toward your goal and unique personal growth.

You'll find places to write out answers, make lists, brainstorm and take notes as you go along. This will help you keep yourself organized and on track as you work through Ms. Hollis' original work. You'll be able to jot down your ideas and how you want to implement them so you can get started faster and easier with your own goal.

Studies show that writing things out helps to solidify learning. You'll want to keep the workbook handy as you move through your goal process, as the information you write down here will prove to be invaluable as you move along.

Most importantly, the workbook was meant to be fun and aid you in your journey toward self-confidence, happiness and personal achievement.

Enjoy the ride!

Background Story of Rachel Hollis

Rachel Hollis is a modern-day trailblazer for women.

At 27, she was named by INC Magazine as one of the "Top 30 Entrepreneurs under 30". She is founder and CEO of her own media company, Chic Media.

She uses her blog and articles to write about the ups and downs of her own experiences to help other women through the problems in their day-to-day lives. She is living proof that it's hard work and persistence that can make your dream come true, even without a college degree or a lot of money.

Ms. Hollis is a New York Times best-selling author for *Girl Wash Your Face*. She said in an interview she wrote the book because she wanted to help all women everywhere who were dealing with similar issues in their life. She wants to help empower women to overcome the obstacles they encounter and understand they have the power to live their dreams.

Introduction: Hey Girl, Hey!

Key Points:

1. No one is responsible for your life but you.
2. Before you start, you have to know where you are.
3. When you believe the lie, you give it power.

Summary/Analysis:

There is one truth this book is about. There is no one on the planet who is responsible for your life but you. You are the one who determines how happy you're going to be. It's up to you. You are responsible for making your life better. If you don't get anything else from this you need to understand that one truth.

But there are roadblocks to understanding that truth. Beliefs that are lies that have gotten in your way. It's important to look at those lies and see how they've shaped your decisions and the choices you've made.

How about the lie that you're too fat? Or the lie that other people are better than you so you should do what they say? Or the lie that because you're not good enough you don't deserve love, so you should accept being treated badly by others?

Every one of those is a lie, and there are a lot more of them, too. Where did they come from? From our upbringing, from what we hear and see on TV and the Internet, from the people we hang out with and from our society's accepted norms.

We've come to accept them and don't even think about them. They've been playing in the background of our lives for so long we don't even realize they're there. But that doesn't make them any less dangerous to our self-esteem and self-worth.

That's why it's so important to take a real look at those lies. To dig deep and identify the lies we've built our lives around. Once we do that, we're on the road to change. When you identify the lie, you understand you can change how you respond to it. And that changes everything.

That's why Ms. Hollis wrote her original work, *Girl, Wash Your Face*. She wants to help women everywhere take a deep look at their own lives and the lies that have been holding them back from becoming who they'd really like to be.

And that's what this workbook is going to help you do by asking the questions you may not have thought about; the questions that will help you get even more from Ms. Hollis' original work. So keep this workbook by your side as you read through her original work so you have a place to jot down all the things that come to you as well as a place to answer the questions we present here.

Ms. Hollis' original work focuses on one big lie for each chapter. One big lie that has caused devastation in the lives of so many women. We'll summarize that here for you and pose questions to help you personalize the information you read in her original work. Those questions can help you dig deep into the lies so you can get past them and turn things around.

You are fabulous, you are strong and you are braver than you give yourself credit for. You can learn and understand move out of the muck the lies have gotten you stuck in.

This is not an overnight process, so don't expect that. It took years of believing in the lies to get to where you are now, so it's going to take some work to turn things around. Remember, this is about your life and how you live it. Every day that you get past another lie is a step forward; a step toward a better today and future.

So get ready to move forward, even if it's only an inch. It's still improvement and it's still heading in the right direction. And that's the whole point.

1. Do you feel responsible for what has happened to you in your life? Why or why not?

_____
_____
_____
_____
_____
_____
_____

2. Can you identify at least three lies that you have built your life around? What are they?

_____
_____
_____
_____
_____
_____
_____

3. Of the three lies you listed in number two, which one has been the hardest for you to deal with? Why?

_____
_____
_____
_____
_____
_____
_____

Chapter One

The Lie: Something Else Will Make Me Happy

Key Points:

1. Stop judging yourself based on how others look.
2. Never give up.
3. Depressed and sad is not the same thing as unhappy.
4. Your happiness is based on who you are, not where you are.

Summary/Analysis:

There isn't anyone anywhere that doesn't have something they'd like to change. Maybe they think their legs are too short, or their hair is too thin. Or their house isn't good enough or they're not good enough.

And why does this happen? Because most people are comparing themselves to other people. We've been raised in a culture that tells us we must be perfect. We must look a particular way, we must act with certain manners, our personality should be comprised of specific characteristics. And it those things don't line up, we're flawed.

Lies, lies, lies!

It's been beaten into our brains to compare our lives to someone else's. And you know what? The very person you're comparing yourself to is probably comparing themselves to someone else. You may think they have it right, but they don't. So your ideal is not ideal at all if you're basing it on someone else.

Unfortunately, women get so frustrated trying to be perfect (which is impossible), they just give up. They give up on themselves and their lives and their hopes and their dreams. Why? Because they believed the lie. And at that point life becomes just getting through the day.

At that point it's a matter of survival, not living. Which means unhappiness settles in. And you don't even know why. You just know you don't feel happy or fulfilled. But, you can't blame that on the other guy or gal or the government or society. Unhappiness is a personal thing. Everyone must take responsibility for their own happiness. It's not up to someone else to do that for you.

We need to stop and define unhappiness here. Unhappiness is not the same thing as being clinically depressed; that's another whole ballgame that requires medical attention. Nor is it just being sad because you've lost a loved one. Again, grief is another story. Sadness and grief have a process you just have to get through.

Here we're talking about being upset about life in general, frustrated with the general path you're on all the related emotions that make you feel like life is barely worth getting through the day.

Stop thinking that someday something magical will happen and then you'll be happy. Stop living your life based on what might happen tomorrow to save you instead of taking action and being responsible today.

Life isn't all of a sudden be perfect because you got a new job or you bought a new house or got a new partner. Those are just more lies. If you're going to be happy, you'll be happy regardless of where you live. You'll find happiness is little things regardless of your job.

Why? Because inside you've chosen to look for the good in life around you. And when you make those inside changes on your perspective, the world looks like a different place. Happiness becomes who you are, not who you're with or what you have. You'll find yourself laughing during a downpour running to the car or smiling at the mess you just made when you spilled your drink. Life just becomes easier.

Happiness isn't something you have to chase. It's something that lives inside you.

Ms. Hollis says there are three things she did that helped her:

Number One: Ms. Hollis stopped comparing herself to the picture she thought she was supposed to be and she stopped comparing herself to other people. Comparison doesn't bring joy, it kills it. If you do your best today, that's enough.

Number Two: Ms. Hollis chose to surround herself with as many things that were positive as she could. If life is always a downer for you, then look around at the people you have in your life and things you do. Who and what you surround yourself with is key.

Number Three: Ms. Hollis took the time to figure out what it was that really made her happy. Maybe it's taking a long hot bath at the end of the day or not filling your schedule with other people's demands. Pay attention and notice what really makes you happy versus what you're doing like a robot to get through the day.

1. Are you comparing yourself to someone else or to a picture of who you think you should be? Who or what is that?

_____
_____
_____
_____
_____
_____
_____

2. Are there negative things in your life you'd like to change? What are they and what positive things can you put in their place?

_____
_____
_____
_____
_____
_____
_____

3. List 5 things that truly make you happy. How can you incorporate those things into your weekly regime?

_____
_____
_____
_____
_____
_____
_____

Chapter Two
The Lie: I'll Start Tomorrow

Key Points:

1. Keep the promises you make to yourself.
2. Society teaches complacency not accountability.
3. When you change your patterns you start to succeed.

Summary/Analysis:

Let's face it, we're made up of our habits. We tend to dress in the same colors, eat the same food, take the same route home from shopping and work.

The same thing applies to keeping true to our promises we make for ourselves. If we're constantly telling ourselves it's okay to not run that mile just for today, or cheat on our diet because we'll make up for it tomorrow, what are we teaching ourselves? What habit are we establishing?

Sure, there will be days when things happen and running that mile at midnight will just be out of the question. The problem happens when we keep breaking that promise to ourselves day after day. When one cheat day on the diet, leads to another and then another until there is no diet at all.

Think about the things you really appreciate in your friends. If your friend tells you they'll be there at 6:00 and they don't show up until 6:30, how happy are you with them? They made a commitment to you and just blatantly broke it with another lame excuse. You'd get to a point where you didn't trust them, right? Would you even want to hang out with them after a while? Probably not.

How different is that when you do it to yourself? When you constantly break the promises you make to yourself you're teaching your subconscious that you can't be counted on to carry through, that you can't be trusted to keep your word. And frankly, that you're flaky.

Can you even count the number of times you didn't keep up your exercise routine because you just didn't feel like it, or you wanted to watch a movie or TV instead? Same thing goes with your diet, etc.

Unfortunately, even our society doesn't teach us to be accountable. Instead, the reasons why it's okay to be complacent abound. The truth is, if you really want to do something you find a way. If you're dying for pizza you'll spend an extra ten minutes and go out of your way to get it.

The same thing is true for wanting to change. If you truly want to get into that new dress for summer, you'll clean out your cupboards, get up early to exercise and take the stairs at work because it's that important to you. You'll push through the old patterns and replace "I'll do it tomorrow" with "I'm doing it right now, regardless, end of story".

And when you do that, something amazing happens. That one small win changes how you look at yourself. You start seeing yourself as someone who can actually get things done and not just think about them. You start to see yourself as successful.

And that small win leads to another and another and another. Because you're changing your patterns. You're pushing through the old negativity into a new way of being. And that's everything. You're acting differently and shaping your life differently.

Some interesting things happen when you start to consciously choose. You won't make promises you can't keep, to yourself or to anyone else. You'll begin to realize how powerful your words are and choose them more carefully. You'll teach yourself how to consciously become the person you want to be.

These are the things Ms. Hollis said helped her:

Number One: Don't try to eat the whole cake all at once. Start with something small like getting up 30 minutes early to exercise three times a week. If your goal is to lose weight, Ms. Hollis recommends setting a goal of drinking half your body weight in water every day. It's easier to add a habit that to take one away. Plus the water will help to fill you up. After you've done that successfully for a month, then move to a more difficult challenge.

Number Two: Don't jump on the bandwagon too soon. It's easy to say yes because something sounds good at the time. But after you think about it you may begin to dread keeping that commitment. Be conscious of what you're committing to and make sure it's really important to you.

Number Three: Self-honesty is everything. If you blow something off, be aware of why you did it and own up to it. Look back at all the things you've bailed on in the last month and become aware of how you've trained yourself to react.

1. What is one small goal you can start with to begin retrain your habits? How would you begin to implement that?

_____
_____
_____
_____
_____
_____
_____

2. Make a list of the commitments you've cancelled on in the last 30 days and why.

_____
_____
_____
_____
_____
_____
_____

3. Looking at the list you just made in #2, honestly evaluate how you've been training yourself to behave.

_____
_____
_____
_____
_____
_____
_____

Chapter Three
The Lie: I'm Not Good Enough

Key Points:

1. Society teaches us we must excel to be worthy.
2. Your emotions affect you physically.
3. Learn how stop and rest to be happy.

Summary/Analysis:

Most of how we learn to act comes from our childhood, from the lessons we learned growing up. And the truth is, what we learn from our childhood affects how we handle ourselves as an adult.

For instance, if we got an A on a spelling test, that was an occasion for praise and adulation. The accomplishment was noted over dinner or relayed to Grandma in a phone conversation and we learned that exceling in matters others felt were important was a good thing and made us feel good about ourselves. We learned it was important to please other people.

But if we came home with a C in Math, even though we tried our hardest, there was no "atta-girl" or acknowledgement of truly trying, but instead an admonishment that we need to do better the next time.

We learned to base our self-worth on what others thought of us and on their values and standards. Striving to meet those goals was important.

For many women that pattern continues on today. Our opinions of ourselves is not so much based on how happy we are with ourselves for all the little things we accomplished today, but on what our bosses or partners think of what we accomplished or didn't accomplish.

How many times have you been so stressed out you got a headache because you were trying to get everything done your boss wanted done that day? Or keep up with all the kid's after-school activities, lessons and educational wants and needs.

That stress can lead to much more than headaches, as you well know. In fact, doctors say that stress is responsible for the majority of ailments they see in their offices today. And who is responsible for accepting all that stress and piling it on top of us? We are.

We are the ones who let ourselves get pushed into doing things we didn't want to do. We are the ones who didn't say "no" when the kids wanted to do one more thing without thinking about how it would affect us (because we wanted to be the "good mom", right?). We are the ones who didn't take a step back and draw the line in the sand and set boundaries.

What kind of example of are we setting for our kids, friends and families when we burn ourselves out like that? What are we teaching ourselves about our own self-worth? Do they see us valuing ourselves and our own needs along with theirs? Or do they see us as a doormat... and what does that teach our kids about their roles when they become an adult?

Learning to rest and take a step back doesn't come overnight, but to be happy and learn to enjoy your life, it's something you need to learn to do.

Maybe you're a mom-aholic or a workaholic, or something-else-aholic. The first thing to do is admit you have a problem overdoing. Then get help from someone who is qualified to help you change and work through it.

Ms. Hollis says these are the things she did to help her deal with being a workaholic:

Number One: She sought help from a qualified therapist. A professional is trained to help you see the connections between the past and the present; connections you may not see on your own. They're also trained to help you develop a workable plan to get through it and change those patterns into constructive ones.

Number Two: Make joy an energy priority. Put as much focus into the fun moments as you do the workaholic moments. If you love walking in the evening, be completely into your walk. Be there with the sunset and the birds chirping and the fresh air. It will do wonders to recharge your batteries and relieve the stress.

Number Three: Re-prioritize your to-do list. If you're like so many women you have your kids, partner, work, faith all on your list. But not you! Your health and needs should be at the very top. You won't be much use to your family and others if you're worn-out from lack of sleep and poor nutrition. That includes how you deal with problems. Make facing them head-on a must instead of running from them.

1. Are you an over-doer? If so, what kind? Be honest with yourself about this.

___

2. What did you learn as a child about your self-worth that has carried on into your adult life? Is that something you want to change and why?

___

3. Write out your priority list. Where are you on that list and why?

___

Chapter Four
The Lie: I'm Better Than You

Key Points:

1. Never judge others. You don't know their story.
2. Accountability comes from love, not judgment.
3. Your truth may not be someone else's.

Summary/Analysis:

Gossip never helps, it only hurts. When we gossip or put the other person down we're not only hurting them, we're doing an injustice to ourselves. People will stop sharing with you because they see you as judgmental and unreliable. They don't want you turning their stories around and retelling them to others.

How many times have you passed judgment on someone, just to find out later you didn't have the whole story? And had you known what was really going on, you would've actually commended that person for doing the best they could under a difficult situation.

Life is not perfect for anyone. Sometimes we have to keep going even when we're in public. Maybe you scoffed at a woman because her dress was too long and baggy. If you'd known that all her clothes were lost in baggage claim and she had to wear a hand-me-down from a friend who wore a different size just to get through, would you have been so mean?

Could there possibly be a correlation to your own past where you didn't have the nicer clothes and this was a way of dealing with your own issues?

Be open-minded and remember you don't know their story and they don't know yours. So leave the judgments behind. We can all learn from each other if we give ourselves a chance. Be as proud of the other person's accomplishments as you would want them to be of yours. You'll find your heart open and that competitive energy lifting instead of dragging you down.

Some people feel that judging is a way of making another person accountable, but is it really? Just because you believe something doesn't mean the other person has to believe it too. You'd be infuriated in you were a Protestant and the other person was a Catholic and condemned you because your faith didn't match theirs.

Ms. Hollis states that accountability comes from love that is developed inside friendships and communities. Judgment comes from hate and fear. Make sure you're not hiding your judgments behind the guise of accountability to make yourself feel better about your own inadequacies.

Ms. Hollis says these were the things that helped her deal with judging:

Number One: Pay attention to the people around you. If they are judgmental and gossip prone you may find yourself adopting their bad habits. If you need to change the people around you, look for positive upbeat people who support and nurture each other.

Number Two: Be your own police. Pay attention to what you say about others or what you think about them. When you find yourself thinking unkind thoughts about someone, immediately stop yourself and come up with something nice that would engender friendship. You'll be doing yourself a huge favor by doing this because you'll be teaching yourself to be positive instead of negative. That makes this a very important exercise in personal development.

Number Three: Be upfront about your own insecurities. When we start pointing fingers and judging it's usually because it touches one of our own issues. Be very honest with yourself about this. If you want to be the best you can, you need to know what has made you think and act the way you do.

1. What do you find yourself judging others about? List at least 5 things.

_____
_____
_____
_____
_____
_____
_____

2. Look at your list from #1 and pick out the biggest issue there. What has happened in your past that makes you so critical of others regarding that issue?

_____
_____
_____
_____
_____
_____
_____

3. List the people you are around the most. How many of their traits do you see in yourself? Is there anything there you'd like to change?

_____
_____
_____
_____
_____
_____
_____

Chapter Five

The Lie: Loving Him Is Enough For Me

Key Points:

1. Don't sacrifice your self-respect for a partner.
2. Self-love sometimes means walking away.
3. You teach people how to treat you by how you value yourself.

Summary/Analysis:

This is one time you must be completely honest with yourself when it comes to your relationships. You must look past the naïve hoping and really look at how you're being treated and what you allow.

You must decide right here and right now that you're going to love yourself and not let another person disrespect you verbally, mentally, emotionally. And neither are you going to let their friends treat you like garbage.

If this is you or has been you, now is the time to open your eyes and see the truth about how you've let yourself down by allowing yourself to be a rug. That doesn't mean berating and demeaning yourself because you were inexperienced or so stuck in your dream world of love to see what was really going on.

Yes, you may be angry at yourself for not seeing the truth earlier and allowing someone to use you. But putting yourself down for something that is over is just a waste of mental and emotional energies. The question is, what did you learn from that and where do you go from here?

Sometimes the most honest thing you can do in a relationship that is not win-win is to walk away. If someone isn't respecting you on all levels you need to understand you've allowed that to happen. If you're not respecting yourself on all levels, then someone else won't respect you either.

That makes walking away the most honest thing you can do for yourself and for the other person as well. When you walk away from a situation like that it shows the other person they need to take a real look at who they are and what they've become as well.

Value of one's self is a part of self-love. A relationship cannot give you self-love. And without self-love, you'll always be wanting, always be looking for it somewhere else; always expecting that hole inside of you to be filled by someone or something or someplace. And it never will. It can only be filled by you.

Every day is a choice. And your choices show your partners and your friends how to treat you. You set the standard.

These are the things Ms. Hollis says would have helped her if she'd only known:

Number One: Find someone you can count on as a sounding board. Maybe it's a minister in your church, a super-wise friend, a professional counselor, it doesn't matter. As long as that person is smart enough to help you see what's going on and how your actions are contributing to the situation. Then guide you with options on how to handle yourself and the situation.

Number Two: Be prepared for the future. If you have kids, the time may come when they need to know what you went through so they don't make the same mistakes. There is a price to pay naivete and lack of self-respect. Your experience may help them raise their self-worth and change how their value themselves.

Number Three: Look at your situation through someone else's eyes. If someone came to you and told you their story and it was full of hurt and disrespect and things you may have gone through, would you say their relationship was healthy? If the answer is an immediate no or you even have to think about it, then it's time to re-evaluate where you stand in your own relationship.

1. Do you feel you are in a healthy relationship? Why or why not?

_____
_____
_____
_____
_____
_____

2. Is there someone you can use as a sounding board regarding your relationship? Who is that person and why would you choose them?

_____
_____
_____
_____
_____
_____

3. Do you feel you love yourself? Why or why not? What could you do to bolster your image of yourself and improve your self-esteem?

_____
_____
_____
_____
_____
_____

Chapter Six

The Lie: No Is The Final Answer

Key Points:

1. No only counts if you accept it
2. How you perceive your reality depends on what happened in your past.
3. When you shift your perception you shift your reality.

Summary/Analysis:

What do you do when someone tells you no? Do you accept it and just say okay? Or do you find an alternative that might solve the problem?

The point Ms. Hollis makes in her original work is that no only means no if you blindly accept it and stop. As long as you accept no without looking for another solution you're going to find the roadblocks in life stopping you. When you find out later there was a detour around that roadblock you're going to end up kicking yourself in the backside because you didn't ask questions and look for other solutions.

Do you have a dream but other people have told you it's impossible? Maybe for them it is impossible. If you let others stop your dream, you're letting them determine who you are and where you can go in life.

That's what's happening when people tell you no and you don't look for another possible solution. You're letting them determine the shape, size and color of your dream. You're giving them control over your life.

Making your life successful isn't just about working hard, or education or how much money you have. It's about hearing no and realizing that just means you may have to change your perspective and find another path to get to where you want to go. No really means slow down, re-evaluate, and look for another path to get to your end point. No doesn't mean stop and forget it.

Yes, perception is reality… to a point. It's the reality of how you think and feel based on what you've learned in your past. But your perception and the other guy's perception of the same situation can be two entirely different things with two completely different outcomes.

Your perception is all about you. It's how you interpret a given set of circumstances based on what you've experienced in the past. If some people come across a washed-out bridge, they turn around and go straight back to where they came from and figure they can't get through. But another guy will see the washed-out bridge, turn around and find another road that goes around that bridge and get to his destination anyway.

If your past tells you you're a loser, nothing ever works out for you so why try, you don't have enough money or time or skill, then that's going to color how you view everything. If you want things to change, then you're going to have to change how you perceive things. You're going to have to move past the old programming and start thinking and doing a different way.

That means you start being grateful. For all the little things everywhere. You start looking for the good instead of blindly accepting the negative voice in your head.

It means you remember why you started out on this journey of a dream and self-improvement in the first place. You find that fire deep inside of you and you grab onto it and you let it override any trauma, drama that's going on around you.

Is that easy? Absolutely not. Is it worth it? Nothing could be more so. Will it take time? Most likely, yes.

Little things come easy; dreams take dedication and work. They take finding alternatives to no. They take pulling that fire up out of the depths of you and telling that negative self-talk yes you can and yes you will.

Do you want the big stuff? If the answer is yes then here is how you get it. You learn to hear "this just means find another way" when life tells you "no".

These are the things Ms. Hollis says helped her:

Number One: Develop some audacity. Not get mean or obnoxious, but learn to ignore the perspectives of other people telling you there's no way you can accomplish your dream. It's considered audacious to ignore the so-called authorities who are telling you what is right for your life. Just remember, it's your life. Learn to go around them.

Number Two: Remember there's more than one path up the side of the mountain. If one path doesn't work to get to the top, find an alternate route. That's all no means… just look for another way.

Number Three: Put your dreams up where you can see them. Use stickies and put them up on the fridge, or cut out pictures and words and put them inside the medicine cabinet door or closet door. Make sure your dream is in front of you every single day. Being fired up in the beginning is easy. Keeping the fire going day after day takes dedication.

1. What do you do when someone tells you no? Why do you think that's so?

_____
_____
_____
_____
_____
_____
_____

2. Are there any limiting beliefs from your past that have programmed you to accept another person's point of view of what is right for you? What are those?

_____
_____
_____
_____
_____
_____
_____

3. What can you do to keep your dream alive in your day-to-day life?

_____
_____
_____
_____
_____
_____
_____

Chapter Seven:
The Lie: I'm Bad At Sex

Key Points:

1. UTI's can happen because of sex.
2. Talk about sex with your partner.

Summary/Analysis:

The first point Ms. Hollis makes in her original work is about UTI's (urinary tract infections). There's a lot about this online and your doctor is another great source of information about this, but the point is: urinate after sex (and before). That one little trick will go a long way to helping to avoid UTIs.

The second major point is this chapter is about doing something you really don't enjoy and not discussing it with your partner. Your partner can tell if you're engaged or not, if you're really enjoying being with them sexually or not. That means they may be feeling emotionally and physically inadequate because they feel you're only doing it please them when you really don't care.

These are the seven steps Ms. Hollis says she took to go from being bad at sex to amazing at it:

Number One: Redefine sex. For many women thinking about sex doesn't really mean it's all positive. What Ms. Hollis did was change how she thought about it. She decided she was going to view sex as fun, not as an obligation. More fun than doing other things like watching TV or read, etc. With that attitude, choosing sex becomes a more enticing choice.

Number Two: If you're uncomfortable with sex you're not enjoying it. Stop and ask yourself what is making you uncomfortable. Now ask yourself what would make you comfortable with sex, make you feel sexy, make you want to engage. The next step is to go to your partner and have an open discussion about all of it. For many women this is embarrassing, but you need to get through it so you and your partner both express yourselves and are working on it together.

Number Three: Ms. Hollis realized part of her issues were due to her religious upbringing as a Christian. She read Hebrews 13:4: "Let marriage be held in honor among all, and let the bed be undefiled".

Ms. Hollis interpreted that to mean that anything that goes on between her and her husband isn't bad as long as it's not harmful to either of them or others. Obviously this excludes pornography, etc. But anything else like role-playing or sexy lingerie is totally acceptable. Again as long as it doesn't hurt either person or others.

Number Four: Change your image of your body. Use positive self-talk when you look at yourself in the mirror instead of telling yourself about any faults you think your body may have. Your partner is just thrilled you're there wanting to be with them and sees your body as exciting at that point.

Number Five: Be committed to your orgasm. Make a decision you're not going to have sex without it. Talk it over with your partner. Most partners are thrilled to hear it since they want to give you pleasure as much as you want to experience it.

Number Six: Figure out what turns you on. Really think about the things that get you going and talk about them with your partner. Experiment and try new things.

Number Seven: Commit to having sex every day for 30 days. Remember this is because you want to, not because you're obligated. Ms. Hollis found that with her commitment to an orgasm with every sexual encounter and doing what really turned her on, this was an amazing time for them both. It was a no-pressure time and gave her the opportunity to try out new things.

1. Do you feel your sex life is what you'd like it to be? Why or why not?

_____
_____
_____
_____
_____
_____
_____

2. If the answer to #1 is no, what about your sex life is making you uncomfortable?

_____
_____
_____
_____
_____
_____
_____

3. What turns you on sexually you're not doing you'd like to discuss and implement with your partner?

_____
_____
_____
_____
_____
_____
_____

Chapter Eight

The Lie: I Don't Know How To Be A Mom

Key Points:

1. You don't have to have it all figured out.
2. Don't try to live up to impossible mom standards you see in the media.
3. Mistakes are going to happen. You're still a good mom.

Summary/Analysis:

This chapter is for the new moms. If you've been a mom for a while and have it down, kudos to you! You probably don't need this.

Being a mom is a day-to-day thing. There is no manual. And there is no such thing as the perfect mom, so don't try to live up to the perfection you think you see in the media. Because it doesn't exist.

Sure at first it's all bliss and excitement because there's a new baby. You have help from parents and friends bring you casseroles to help you through the first week or two. But then you find yourself on your own with your partner being a new mom and you start to think of everything that could go wrong. Don't do that.

Ms. Hollis says there are only two things you need to do to be a good mom:

1. Take care of your baby.
2. Take care of yourself.

That's it. If you do this two things, you're doing great. If the baby is fed, dry, loved cuddled and clean, you're doing great for him/her. If you've managed a shower, eaten well, rested as much as you can and taken care of yourself to the best of your ability, bravo. You're a good mom.

If the living room didn't get vacuumed but you managed those two things, that's okay. The vacuuming can wait.

Don't let the media overwhelm you with needing the perfect nursery, the perfect homemade organic baby food, keeping your baby on the perfect schedule, etc. There are so many books out there about doing all the so-called right things you can make yourself crazy imagining all the things that could go wrong.

If you're driving yourself nuts about all those things, guess what? You're a loving, concerned mom. Everything will fall into place and be fine.

Things that helped Ms. Hollis:

Number One: Find your tribe. Maybe it's a group oriented especially toward moms, or a church group or a special yoga class for moms and their little ones. Look around and find one that works for you. It's very helpful to have someone to talk to who's going through the same things you are and can understand where you're at.

Number Two: Take a break from social media. All the pictures you feel are of the perfect life can make you feel like you're doing everything wrong and you're not. If going online and looking at social media posts stresses you out and makes you anxious, then leave it alone for a while. Use that time to give yourself a much-needed rest and relax instead.

Number Three: Make sure you do this every day, not every week. Get out of the house every day. Take baby for a walk in their stroller and get out there and away from any stress you're feeling at home. What's important is you realize there is life beyond the four walls of your home and you're still part of the outside world.

Number Four: Voice what's bothering you. Keeping your feelings bottled up isn't going to help. Choose someone supportive you can trust and talk about the things you're struggling with. Doing that can help you understand the lies that are stressing you and help you see you're handling things much better than you thought.

1. Are you a new mom? What is your biggest challenge?

_____
_____
_____
_____
_____
_____

2. Do you feel you are taking care of yourself? Why or why not?

_____
_____
_____
_____
_____
_____

3. Do you have a tribe? If yes, who are they and how do you get help there? If not, where can you go to find a tribe of new moms?

_____
_____
_____
_____
_____
_____

Chapter Nine

The Lie: I'm Not A Good Mom

Key Points:

1. Forget trying to be someone else's perception of a mom.
2. If you need help from others, ask for reinforcements.
3. Don't compare your family to other families.

Summary/Analysis:

Just because the other moms can be at all the school functions, volunteer for lots of committees and be there for every classroom event doesn't mean you have to.

They have different work commitments, different lifestyles, different perspectives, different time commitments and on and on.

Whatever the differences are doesn't really matter. If you're loving your kids and doing the best you can do for them and for yourself you're a good mom. You need to make life work for you and family, not try to meet the standards of someone else's lifestyle. If they were leading your life, they might be making the exact same choices you are.

There are going to be up days being a mom and down days. Some days everything will flow, other days you'll wonder who replaced your kids with little monsters. Every family is unique with different needs. Do what works for you and yours.

Remember, this isn't just about your kids, it's about you, too. You have needs and they're just as important as your kids'. That means there are going to be times when you need a break away from them, time to just be you without constant interruption. Let's face it, there are going to be days when you're at your wits end and just need some personal downtime.

That's when you ask for help. Call your mom, a best friend, take the kids to a supervised playland, whatever works for you. Go do things you love to do but rarely have time for. Maybe get your hair done and get mani-pedi, or go to the park and relax and read in a nice little shady spot. If you can work it out, try to get away for an entire day or the weekend.

Little breaks like that can relieve so much stress and change your entire attitude. Just imagine taking a nap in the middle of the day, sleeping in, going for a leisurely walk… all without guilt or drama. You absolutely need downtime for yourself if you want to stay sane and be of service to yourself and to your kids.

Things Ms. Hollis says helped her:

Number One: The evidence says it all. Instead of telling yourself everything you're doing wrong, look at the kind of kids you've raised. Are they kind to other people, do well in school, well-mannered in public? Then you've done a good job. But, if they're in trouble at school all the time, mean to others and rude to you, then you may want to seek help. As long as they're basically good human beings most of the time, stop criticizing yourself and realize you're doing just fine as a mom.

Number Two: Become friends with the other moms. They're doing the exact same thing you were doing… comparing themselves to the other moms. They're just as worried they're doing the wrong things as you are. The more you realize you're all having the same issues, the more you realize you're okay and not the worst mom on the block.

Number Three: Go for quality. When you're doing things with your kids, don't be doing three other things at the same time. Stay away from the computer and the phone and enjoy them. Play a game with them, take them to the movies, let them help with dinner, etc. Real quality time of being in the moment with them will feel like magic to all of you.

1. Do you feel like you are a good mom? Why or why not?

_____
_____
_____
_____
_____
_____

2. Do you take breaks for yourself away from the kids? If not, what can you plan to change that?

_____
_____
_____
_____
_____
_____

3. Do you spend quality time with your kids? What do you do with just them? Is there anything you'd like to add or change about that?

_____
_____
_____
_____
_____
_____

Chapter Ten

The Lie: I Should Be Further Along By Now

Key Points:

1. Goals don't have expiration dates.
2. Take your focus off the absence of things.
3. Give yourself credit for what you have done.

Summary/Analysis:

Many women are not thrilled about the passing of another birthday. Not because they feel they're growing older, but because of a dream that never happened.

May they thought they'd have a big bank account and be retired by a certain age, but are still working. Or they'd have a big home on the beach, but are still living in suburbia. The list goes on and on. And so they judge themselves because of what they thought their life would be instead of what their life is.

We forget there are hundreds of things involved we have no knowledge of. Maybe the timing is wrong or we just haven't made the right connections yet. Or maybe you're just going through the in-between steps that are going to get there you after all.

Negative self-talk about everything you don't have is a real bummer. It can take you down faster than anything.

What about all the things you have accomplished? What about that great kid you're raising who's a good human being? Or all the time you give to others and your family holding their hand when they're having a bad day? Those are not little things and have immeasurable value in the lives that you've touched.

You've accomplished hundreds of things you've not given yourself credit for. Big and little things. Little things are steps to bigger things and they count. Celebrate them and give yourself a pat on the back.

Things that helped Ms. Hollis:

Number One: Make a list of all the things you've done. Use as much paper and take as much time as you need. When you see down in black and white it makes a big difference. Then write a letter to yourself about how strong and brave you truly are. Believe me, that letter can be a game changer. Keep it handy and read it when you're going through a bad day. It can help bring you back again.

Number Two: Talk over how you feel with someone. Let's face it, we're often embarrassed to tell someone we feel like a complete and utter failure. After all, who wants to openly admit that to someone? That's just a chance for someone to confirm what we're feeling, right? Wrong. That person is going to roll their eyes and tell you remember all the things that are going right and you have accomplished. So find someone to help you talk through things and remember that.

Number Three: Forget the time limits when it comes to your goals. Goals are great because they can help you stay focused. But don't put an end date on them. As long as you're basically moving forward you're heading in the right direction. So a month, a year, ten years... it's all good.

1. Make a list of your accomplishments big and little. Keep it handy and add to it each week to remind yourself of how much you're really doing.

_____
_____
_____
_____
_____
_____
_____

2. Write a letter to yourself about how much strength, perseverance and tenacity you really have. Make sure you keep it and read it through on the down days to bring you back.

_____
_____
_____
_____
_____
_____
_____

3. Do you have someone you can talk to about how you're feeling? Who is that person? If not, who could that person be?

_____
_____
_____
_____
_____
_____
_____

Chapter Eleven

The Lie: Other People's Kids Are So Much Cleaner/Better Organized/More Polite

Key Points:

1. Embrace your chaos.
2. Take a break.
3. Accept help when it's offered.

Summary/Analysis:

Very few people are living a quiet peaceful life without drama and chaos. In this world of multi-tasking moms chaos just goes with the territory.

Most people deal with chaos in one of three ways:

Way Number One: Just ignore it. This is one of the most common ways to deal with chaos. Pretend it isn't there and just keep plowing through.

Unfortunately this method can also be quite stressful, leading to any number of physical side-effects like hives, headaches, insomnia, etc.

Way Number Two: We war and battle against it. We super-clean the bathroom and the kitchen. Then we go on window-washing binge. After that we're looking at the kids with a microscope and making sure their ears are clean, their hair is brushed and they've stayed clean for at least the last hour.

We do everything we can to make it look like life is calm and perfect. Why? Because if everything on the outside of us looks serene and ordered then maybe we'll be peaceful on the inside. We're looking for control.

The problem with battling is that you never win. We embrace a mindset that says if we organize everything well enough, if we plan things out perfectly and plan for every contingency, then things will go according to schedule. Doesn't work.

Way Number Three: Let the chaos drown us. This is where overwhelm comes in. Overwhelmed by the kids activity schedules, by work, by housework, requests from our families, etc.

We start down the road by complaining about every little thing. Negativity becomes a way of life. Eventually we forget how to look for the good in the blessings we do have.

You are more than this. Look around you. You have kids to raise, financial obligations, and a life you can live and make better if you're not ducking the issue.

All three of these ways can lead to even bigger issues like over-eating, drinking, even drugs. Those are all coping mechanisms and unfortunately, you can get drawn into them without even realizing you could be developing a dangerous habit.

So what is the alternative then? If not drowning in chaos, ignoring it or battling it, what else is there? Accepting it.

Yes, that's right. You heard me correctly. Just accept it. Stop going against the tide and float along with it. There is beauty in anything and that includes the chaos. Even laughter and hugs when you change how you perceive and deal with.

Next question… just exactly how do you embrace chaos? Good question. First you start by cutting yourself some slack. Don't freak out when you forget something on your to-do list and things have all of a sudden gone upside down.

Stop, take a deep breath and remember you're doing the best you can. You couldn't have done it any better in the moment; hindsight is not living in the now so forget beating yourself up.

If you can take a moment to take a softer look at the chaos you may just find yourself smiling. Take a moment and make yourself look for the humor in the situation. It may not be easy at first, but eventually you'll get there.

And, dare I say it again, take a break. You need some time to yourself so you can get away and decompress. This is so important. Once you reconnect with the outside world and fill your energy back up, it's much easier to deal with the chaos when you go back. It looks less important and so much less dramatic.

Things that helped Ms. Hollis:

Number One: Find friends in your same boat. In other words, if you're a stay-at-home mom with three kids in grade school, fine other moms in your similar situation. If you're a working mom who relies on sitters and after-school care to get through, find other working moms like you. Being able to talk to others going through similar life situations is not only being able to vent on each other's shoulders, it's also a source of encouragement to help get you through the day.

Number Two: Figure out your priorities. What's the most important thing to you? Not what your mother-in-law feels is most important, but what matters most to you. Maybe it's running a 10K, keeping the house spotless, finishing your degree, or any number of other things. Write it out. Then take it on one thing at a time. Don't try to do it all at once. If you're top priority is finishing your degree, then running the 10K may have to wait.

Number Three: Special treat time. Find something that helps you unwind. Running, watching a special TV program or movie, cooking a gourmet meal… something you consider an indulgence. A happy place for you to retreat to when the overwhelm is at your door.

1. Do you have friends you can talk to who are in the same situation you are? Who are they? If not, how would you plan on meeting like-minded people?

_____
_____
_____
_____
_____
_____

2. Sit down and write out your priorities for yourself. Decide what is truly most important and which things can wait.

_____
_____
_____
_____
_____
_____

3. Do you have a happy place or special treat you can indulge in to decompress? What is that? If not, what could you create to fill that need?

_____
_____
_____
_____
_____
_____

Chapter 12

The Lie: I Need To Make Myself Smaller

Key Points:

1. Get inspiration and help from multiple source.
2. You can't be big and small at the same time.
3. Embrace your whole self, even if it makes others uncomfortable.

Summary/Analysis:

Always be looking for ways to grow and learn. Look for help and information from podcasts, classes, conferences, books, etc. Don't limit yourself to just one source of inspiration.

We're all multi-faceted and no one person is going to have all the answers we need. We change and grow every single day, so what you used to consider the gospel from someone last year may not feel right now. So branch out and keep an open mind.

Don't be afraid to delve deep and ask yourself questions you may have never asked yourself before. Ms. Hollis talks about attending a conference where she was asked two things:

1. Which parent did she crave love from the most? Not the one she loved the most but the one she needed the love from the most.
2. Who did she have to be for them?

For many women part of the answer may be that to get that parent's attention and approval you needed to be seen and not heard as a child. You needed to play quietly and not make a fuss or you might lose the approval. You needed to make yourself small… stay the "little girl".

If you've gone through similar situations then being the "little girl" became being the "little woman". Putting your achievements into smaller frameworks so they didn't override being a mother and wife.

When asked what you do for a living you'd say you had a hobby of writing when in reality you'd written several books doing quite well and were almost finishing another.

You learned not to boast or be proud. Being boastful was something men did. Talking of achievements and how well you were doing was something for men, not for women.

Women learned to mute themselves, what they'd accomplished and any dreams they had. We were taught to stay small and not be boastful.

We're talking about fear. Fear to dream, fear to let accomplishments shine, fear to let go and speak up for yourself. Why? Because we might ruffle some feathers. Our mother-in-law wouldn't approve or maybe our parents would give us that look that says, "Oh, really? Just who do you think you are?"

So you stopped pushing yourself to the next level and held back and stayed quiet because it was safe.

You do not have to choose between being a good mom and raising your kids and having your dream job, or training for the marathon or finishing your degree. You can be just as forthright as a man and just as honest about being you… all of you.

Never lose yourself in someone else's idea of who you should be. No one else can decide that for you unless you let them.

Things that helped Ms. Hollis:

Number One: Be willing to offend. No offend as in telling crude jokes or openly insulting someone. But accept the idea that not everyone needs to approve of you or even like you. For people-pleasers this is a hard one. Stop focusing on what everyone else might say or think. Instead, be the best you can be in any given situation. And if the other person doesn't approve, then that's their issue and none of your business.

Number Two: Make a bold statement. If there's a personal statement you've been holding back on, now is the time to do it. Maybe you wanted to change your hair color or hair style but were afraid of what your family or friends would say.

We choose to be the person that's looking back at us in the mirror. Whether that be a salesperson, or attorney or stay-at-home mom, we made choices that put us where we are today.

Number Three: Listen to some speakers/gurus. You don't have to do everything you hear them say, but often times you can glean some valuable information that can help you push to the next level. Don't get stuck on just one. You need various perspectives. If you're muting yourself branch out and start listening to people who can help you ask the hard questions that lead to deep personal growth.

1. Are you willing to unmute yourself and say and be who you really are? Why or why not?

_____
_____
_____
_____
_____
_____
_____

2. Is there some personal statement you've been longing to make, but afraid of what others would say about it? What is that?

_____
_____
_____
_____
_____
_____
_____

3. Do you have gurus and/or speakers you can listen to for inspiration and breaking through being small? Who are they? How do you intend to find others as well?

_____
_____
_____
_____
_____
_____
_____

Chapter 13

The Lie: I'm Going To Marry Matt Damon

Key Points:

1. Fantasies can help you get to your goal.
2. Break your dreams down into smaller bites.
3. Write. It. Down.

Summary/Analysis:

We've all had the big heart-throb crushes growing up. The ones where we see ourselves married to some super-star having their kids and living this incredible life. Of course, those are fantasies we usually have in our teen-age years, but still at the time, they consumed us in our dreams.

Which brings us to the next points. Fantasies can help you accomplish your goals. Sure, the fantasy itself may not happen the way you imagined it, but the fact that you're invested in it emotionally and mentally is painting a picture in your mind. And that movie you're playing in is shaping your reality.

Sure, you're not going to end up married to your version of Matt Damon, but that dreaming and planning may have lead you to a college course you may not have otherwise considered. And that lead to a college degree you would never have otherwise pursued.

The problem with making dreams so super-huge is they don't seem real to us. They don't seem like it's anything that can really be accomplished. And when that happens we give up.

But if you were to take that dream and break it down into smaller bites, then it would feel completely different.

Let's say you want to be a doctor but the idea of going through eight years of college while raising a family is just over the top. But, taking just one class this semester and one in the summer and one in the fall is completely doable.

And when the kids get older and can take care of themselves more and help out around the house, you might be able to take two classes a semester and so on. And before you know it, you've achieved your first four-year degree.

Here's the trick. Write it down. Leave nothing out. Every single detail. What are the smells in your dream? How is everyone dressed? How are you feeling? Do it every day. The scenarios are going to change from day-to-day because you're building and growing with the dream. This is so powerful. But you have to actually do it to understand and get the magic from it.

It doesn't matter if your fantasy is silly. It gives you something positive to think about and rev-up your imagination with. And it does wonders to keep you focused and motivated.

Things that helped Ms. Hollis:

Number One. Writing everything down. Yes, I know we've said it before, but this one is a biggee and did wonders for Ms. Hollis. You're dreaming of things for yourself that you want and keep your motivated and moving forward. Just do it. It works.

Number Two: Say your dreams out loud. Be clear and make it positive and in the now. Say to yourself, "I am getting my medical degree", instead of, "I want to go back to school".

Say it when you're taking a shower, out running errands, anyplace where you can talk to yourself and not be heard. You don't want someone else making fun of you or your dream declaration. You're making a statement that this is going on right now, not that it's out in the future somewhere.

Number Three: Vision boards. This can be a lot of fun. You're going to make a collage of the things that make your dream feel real to you. Maybe you have a college hat on your board and a stethoscope and a picture of a doctor helping a little girl. If you don't feel your imagination is that strong, this can be of great benefit. Even use words like "strong", "courageous", "helpful", "kind". Whatever fits your particular dream.

1. Did you have a dream that you thought about intently when you were younger? Did it really happen? What did that dream help you accomplish in your life by just thinking about it?

_____
_____
_____
_____
_____
_____

2. What are your dreams now? Is there one you've been holding back on? What is it?

_____
_____
_____
_____
_____
_____

3. How can you break the big dream in #2 down into smaller bites? What are some steps you could start to implement today?

_____
_____
_____
_____
_____
_____
_____

Chapter Fourteen

The Lie: I'm A Terrible Writer

Key Points:

1. What someone else thinks of you is none of your business.
2. Don't make the mistake of validating your work based on someone else's standards.
3. Your art is a personal and spiritual experience.

Summary/Analysis:

We're going to say this again and make a big point of it. What other people think of you has nothing to do with you. They're judging your work because they have a set of standards you do not. They've had experiences you have not had. So, in their eyes, based on their life, your art form... whatever it is... isn't up to snuff. That's okay.

We all do it. We see something someone else has done and we don't like it. Why? Because our past experiences have told us it isn't good enough. Do you really think that person should stop everything they're doing just to please you? I highly doubt it. You voice your opinion in whatever manner you're voicing it and you move on. You don't change your life because you didn't like their work. And neither should they. Because that's your business, not theirs.

If you spend your life wondering why someone doesn't like your painting or your writing or the way you raise your kids you'll nowhere real fast. All your time and energy will be going into building a huge drama around not being liked by that person instead of going into your art or your dream.

Is it worth losing yourself and your dream? No. Would you want to be responsible for someone else giving up on themselves and their dream because you didn't like their painting? Absolutely not. You'd feel awful. Now do you get it?

Art and life itself is a personal experience as well as a spiritual one. For many artists it's about baring their soul into an expression they can feel and touch. The same goes for a particular lifestyle you've chosen. It's more than something you're doing. It's a piece of you from down deep you're expressing in a physical world.

So keep your inner light burning. Express your soul in your art and your life. It's a beautiful thing.

Things that helped Ms. Hollis:

Number One: Stop reading reviews. We all get reviewed whether we're writers or not. Stop seeking them out. Let those people express their needs however they need to. They're not doing it for you; they're doing it for themselves. It's their business. Leave it alone.

Number Two: Write for you. Writing is a creative outlet. Any art is a creative outlet. It's you being you. For many artists, the ability to express themselves as a writer or painter, etc., is a dream that they're living. That makes it sacred to them. You may express your creativity if any number of ways. Always remember, it's a gift. Treat it with respect and never allow the other guy to take it from you with their opinion.

Number Three: Go silly. Let go and color outside the lines of life. Forget the rules and laugh out loud, wear new colors, sing around the house just because it feels good. Do it just because it feels good and makes you happy.

1. Have you allowed someone else's opinion stopped you from accomplishing a goal? What was that opinion and what was the goal?

_____
_____
_____
_____
_____
_____

2. Do you have a creative outlet? What is it? How is it helping you to open up and reach deeper?

_____
_____
_____
_____
_____
_____

3. Do you take time to be silly? Why or why not? How can you expand on that openness?

_____
_____
_____
_____
_____
_____
_____

Chapter Fifteen:
I Will Never Get Past This

Key Points:

1. Embrace the good side of trauma as well as the bad.
2. You can come out on the other side of trauma and thrive.
3. Learn to find purpose without explanation.

Summary/Analysis:

Everyone has their story of trauma. Which means it was devastating and colored our lives in many ways. Many have never really gotten over it and still harbor the anger, resentment and fear that came with it.

We're not trying to make light of anyone's trauma. The message is not to give in to it and let it continue to control you and your life. The trauma can only take away your dream of who you want to be if you let it.

What Ms. Hollis discovered in a Tony Robbins' documentary called "*I'm Not Your Guru*" is just this (in his words): "If you're going to blame your hard times for all the things that are wrong in your life, you better also blame them for the good stuff too!"

Finding the good in a trauma is not what we've been taught to do. Sure, we blame the trauma for all the hard times, insecurities, bad decisions and so on, but how many times do we look at the trauma and find the strengths and path changes that have led to amazing people and experiences had that not happened?

How many times have you been up against a tough situation and reminded yourself if you could get through that past trauma you can absolutely get through this? That's strength. That's perseverance. And believe it or not, that's a gift from that very bad time in your life.

And you did it. You got through another tough situation and you did it with all the grace and power that you could. And you added more confidence to your character and to your mindset than you had before.

Trauma will swallow you up if you let it. It will keep rising up in your consciousness to remind you of the pain and suffering you went through. But the more you tell it you're stronger than that, the less chance it will have of pulling you under.

Maybe things happen for a reason and maybe they don't. What really matters is you find purpose in rising up past the bad into the good for no particular reason other than you can.

Things that helped Ms. Hollis:

Number One: Therapy. Yes, this was talked about before. But, this is another instance where speaking with a professional you have confidence in can be invaluable. That doesn't mean it's going to be easy. But if that person can get you past the haunting memories, it's going to be worth it.

Number Two: Talk it out with someone you trust. With someone else besides your therapist. Maybe it's your partner or your best friend or a member of your family. Talking through all those details can help release the bottled-up burden you've been carrying inside.

Number Three: Set up five minutes to think about it. This may sounds crazy, but it works. It works because it tells your mind you're going to give it five whole minutes every day to think about all the things that keep going round and round in your mind. Five minutes to vent and release it all. Set a timer.

Doing this gives you control of your mind and how and when you're going to think about it instead of being stuck in an uncontrolled loop. Try it; it works.

1. Do you have a past trauma that keeps coming back to haunt you? What is it?

_____
_____
_____
_____
_____
_____

2. What have you done to help yourself through the trauma? Have you seen a therapist? Why or why not?

_____
_____
_____
_____
_____
_____

3. List the good things that have happened to you because you experienced that trauma. What are the gifts?

_____
_____
_____
_____
_____
_____
_____

Chapter Sixteen

The Lie: I Can't Tell The Truth

Key Points:

1. Stay the course.
2. Dreams don't vanish because things are hard.
3. Believe in yourself and your spirit.

Summary/Analysis:

Stress and heartbreak are two of the worst things you can put together. There is so much pain and suffering that comes from those times you don't know how you're going to get through it.

In this chapter Ms. Hollis bravely tells us of the ordeal she and her family went through in their efforts to adopt a baby girl. And while Ms.

Hollis understands the need for all the rules, what she and her family went through was one of the worst times of their lives.

But through all the tears and the sadness and the difficulties, she was able to pull herself together by relying on her spiritual upbringing and her belief in God. She credits those things with her ability to endure such a difficult time.

There are going to be tough times. But you have to keep showing up. You have to keep telling yourself yes... you can do this. And you must always remember there is a light at the end of the tunnel. You may not see it while you go through the drama, but it's there. And you will get to it.

Things that helped Ms. Hollis:

Number One: Be honest with what's happening. This may sound easy, but often it is not. It can be downright unpleasant and scary. But once you start to live in honesty, the easier it becomes.

Number Two: Find a community of truth tellers. There are others like you who have come forth with their stories and been completely honest about their stories. They can help you to find and stay in your own strength. They can show you that living through hardship is possible and you can do it, too.

Number Three: Research. Ms. Hollis feels if they'd done more research in the beginning before taking on the adoption process, they wouldn't have been so shocked with the proceedings.

Do your research before you take on major life-altering changes. Find others going through the process you're undertaking. This will help tremendously in alleviating the feeling of being alone with no one understanding what you're going through.

1. Is there something in your past you still feel so traumatized by you feel you can't tell the truth about it? What is it?

_____
_____
_____
_____
_____
_____

2. Have you ever taken the plunge and decided to open up about the trauma in #1? Did that help you and how?

_____
_____
_____
_____
_____
_____

3. Are you involved in a community of other truth-tellers? If yes, who are they and how has that helped you? If not, what steps can you take to find such a group?

_____
_____
_____
_____
_____
_____

Chapter Seventeen

The Lie: I Am Defined By My Weight

Key Points:

1. It's the care you put into your body that says more about you than your weight.
2. Stop making excuses for staying stuck and not taking care of yourself.
3. Self-love starts with your physical body.

Summary/Analysis:

We've been programmed to think if we have a certain look, if the scale shows a certain weight, then life will magically change and we'll get the life we've been wanting.

So we go through multiple diets, take diet pills and try every diet craze that's out there. All in the attempt to become the person we see in the magazines and in the media.

We use childhood trauma, loss of jobs and loved ones and any number of other things as an excuse to use food as a coping mechanism. Which is fine in the short-term, but not as a lifestyle.

None of these things are a life sentence. At some point you have to stop making excuses as to why you're abusing your body. You're making a choice. If you continue to overeat for whatever reason you've convinced yourself is valid, you're making a choice to abuse your body.

Forget about how much you weigh. Look at your body. What kind of food are you eating? Is it mostly junk food or whole nourishing foods? Are you drinking plenty of fluids? Are you giving you muscles and bones the excise they need to stay strong?

You don't need to be a certain size or a certain weight. But you do need to love yourself enough to take care of your body. That's what defines you, not the numbers looking back at you on the scales.

This is not an overnight thing. If you're overweight and out of shape, you've made choices that made that happen. That means you have the power to make different choices and change that.

Bottom line is, you need to burn more calories than you take in if you want to lose weight. You need to exercise to stay strong emotionally, mentally and physically.

Self-love starts in your body. It doesn't get any more personal than that.

Things that helped Ms. Hollis:

Number One: Use mantra to change the voice in your head. Poor self-image comes from negative self-talk. Walking around all day berating yourself makes you feel and believe you're not good enough and never will be. Find a mantra that is the opposite of that negative self-talk and say it to yourself all day, every day. Maybe it's, "I'm strong, I'm healthy, I'm smart." Or maybe it's, "I'm a good mom, I'm happy, I'm beautiful." Make it fit what works for you. And repeat it all day every day until it becomes your reality.

Number Two: Stop choosing media that makes you feel inferior. If every time you look at pictures of models on Instagram, stop following them. If you get depressed every time you open People magazine, stay away from it. There may be a time and a place for that later, but not when you're in the middle of updating your self-image. Follow people who are healthy and happy. Read about women who are strong and courageous. Surround yourself with images of women who make you feel hopeful.

Number Three: Be prepared. Don't wait until the last minute to figure out how you're going to get yourself into a healthier lifestyle. If you know you want to get to the gym to the exercise, then get out your planner and schedule it in. Get your workout clothes ready and set an alarm to make sure you get yourself there as scheduled.

If you're trying to lose weight, then make sure you have healthy snacks around. Take the time to fix them and have them ready to grab instead of cookies and crackers. Make it a priority to take care of yourself.

1. Do you have negative self-talk going on in your head? If yes, what is it?

_____
_____
_____
_____
_____
_____
_____

2. Write out a mantra you can use to turn the negative self-talk identified in #1 around.

_____
_____
_____
_____
_____
_____
_____

3. What preparations can you make to help you move forward with a healthy of self-care?

_____
_____
_____
_____
_____
_____
_____

Chapter Eighteen

The Lie: I Need A Drink

Key Points:

1. There's nothing wrong with you; there's nothing to medicate.
2. Build up your emotional/mental immune system and you can survive and thrive.
3. Find new habits to deal with stress.

Summary/Analysis:

Grabbing a drink is an easy fix. It can take the edge off and stop you from screaming at your kids and going over the edge. It helps you through those times when you feel there's something wrong with you, so you need to medicate yourself with alcohol to deal with your shortcomings and get through.

Thousands of women feel there's something wrong with them. That they're falling short and the alcohol will help deal with those shortcomings. The truth is, there's nothing wrong with you. You're a real mom going through real problems that thousands of other women are going through, too. You're not broken.

Drinking alcohol is so easy, which is why it's hard to stop. It's an easy fix to all the stress and drama. Alcohol makes it so easy to zone out once the kids are in bed and let yourself float away.

There's only one way to healthily deal with stress, and that's to build up your mental/emotional immune system. The stress you deal with today makes you stronger and smarter for the next time it comes up. So when the situation arrives in the future you know what to do and how to do it.

And each different drama produces another stress that you learn to cope with and handle. So if it pops up again, you'll not be devastated because you did it before and this time you know what to do.

Build yourself a new habit to deal with stress. Maybe it's exercising or hanging out with your friends. Maybe it's seeing a counselor or soaking and having a good cry. You're an individual and what works for someone else may not work for you. Try different things and come up with a new way to handle it.

Only you know where you stand with this whole issue. If your first reaction is to run for a drink or a pill or your drug of choice, then you're looking for a quick fix.

Building inner strength takes time. It won't happen overnight, but it will happen if you choose it.

Things that helped Ms. Hollis:

Number One: Learn about your habits. They are triggered by cues... things that we feel, experience, etc., that set us off. Pay attention to what sets off your bad habit. That's your cue. Now find new coping mechanisms like running or getting together with your friends to deal with it.

Number Two: Accept your reality. Become self-aware. You can't fix the problem if you don't look at it for what it really is. Once you uncover the weakness for what it is, you can start finding answers to head toward strength.

Number Three: Get the trigger out of your house. If you have alcohol in the house and that's a problem for you, dump it. If you binge-eat, throw out the cakes and candy and junk food. No, it won't solve the whole problem, but it will make dealing with it easier.

1 How do you deal with stress? Is there anything about that you'd like to change?

_____
_____
_____
_____
_____
_____
_____

2. What are you negative habits? Do you know what cues/triggers set them off? What are they?

_____
_____
_____
_____
_____
_____

3. List three ways you can deal with stress in a positive way without drugs, alcohol, binge-eating, etc.

_____
_____
_____
_____
_____
_____
_____

Chapter Nineteen

The Lie: There's Only One Right Way To Be

Key Points:

1. You're more alike others than you are different.
2. Diversity makes you a stronger better version of yourself.
3. Make your community soul-deep instead of skin-deep.

Summary/Analysis:

So many women have grown up in communities where everyone was pretty much alike. Same skin color, same religious beliefs, same income class. Unfortunately, if we maintain those same qualities as an adult, we're narrowing our perspectives and opportunities to grow.

The other big problem with not moving outside the box is judgment. There is the tendency to judge others who aren't like us. If we stopped to meet others and listen to their story we'd probably find they're dealing with the same things we are. We'd also get to hear their stories of courage and heart and have the opportunity to expand who we are and learn from them. And that is the point. To become better versions of ourselves.

The world is so diversified with so much to offer. Think of it as an ice cream store with 35 flavors vs. an ice cream store with only 3 flavors. The ice cream store with 3 flavors is the community you grew up in. It's all you knew as a child.

The ice cream store with 35 flavors is the world outside of your community. If you don't get outside of the box and try the other 32 flavors how do you know if you like them or not? Maybe you'd even like them better than the original 3 flavors you knew growing up.

Trying new things expands our minds and our soul. It let's us experience other perspectives and challenge our thoughts and beliefs. And that's where real opportunity comes in. The opportunity to be a brighter, happier, better version of who we'd like to be.

Getting outside of that box into a larger more diverse community lets you make friends you can relate to on a deeper level that goes past their color, religion and sexual preference. You experience them on a soul-level that goes beyond the surface.

That's doesn't mean you changing everything you've ever believed in. It means you're expanding your perspective and awareness to see people with a broader, more open way of thinking. And giving them the opportunity to view you without bias and judgment as well.

Things that helped Ms. Hollis:

Number One: Changing Churches. Ms. Hollis realized the church she was attending was almost completely white. She sought out a church that embraced all cultures, races and generations and found real community.

Number Two: Own up to your present perspective. Look at your beliefs. Look at the people you surround yourself with. If they look and believe almost exactly as you do, then it's time to diversify. Get outside of your box and find new experiences and forge new friendships.

Number Three: Ask questions humbly. If you have a friend from another race or culture, humbly ask them questions about their background and any cultural/racial bias so you don't offend others with your ignorance. First ask your friend if they would be offended by discussing those things with you. And again, be humble in your conversations and questions. You're asking another being to let you walk a mile in their shoes.

1. Look around you. What does your current community look like economically, socially, ethnically?

_____
_____
_____
_____
_____
_____
_____

2. Refer to your answer in #1. Is your community diversified? If not, what would you like your community to look like?

_____
_____
_____
_____
_____
_____
_____

3. Think about your current belief system. Do you have beliefs that limit your growth and interacting with other cultures? What are they?

_____
_____
_____
_____
_____
_____
_____

Chapter Twenty

The Lie: I Need A Hero

Key Points:

1. Look in the mirror; that's your hero.
2. Set a goal right now and do it.
3. Stop the self-drama and start over today.

Summary/Analysis:

You've done more than you think you have. You've raised your kids, gotten through sleepless nights, dealt with overbearing critical people who judged you for no reason, slugged your way through endless relationship issues and found a way to get up the next morning and keep going.

You. You did that. Not someone else.

All your achievements, big and little, that's all you. Not some mythical legend out of a book or a movie, you. And every one of those accomplishments helped you to build your life, change it, grow it, be it.

The power is in your hands right here, right now. It never was anywhere else and it never will be. The power to be the dream you keep thinking about. The power to do the things you've been longing to do.

Stop looking around for someone else to be your hero. Really look at your courage and your tenacity. Your endurance and your strength. Really look at you.

Set a goal for yourself, something you can strive and work toward. Something to put that strength and determination into. To help consciously build your belief in yourself.

The goal can be anything. Running a half-marathon, losing that last five pounds, finishing that college degree, it doesn't matter. Set the goal and do it. This is about proving your worth to yourself. It's showing yourself and the world you can do anything you choose to do.

Stop waiting for the other guy to fix your life. You'll be waiting forever. No one can fix you but you. You got yourself where you are today. You can get yourself where you want to be for tomorrow. Your power. Your choices.

If you want your life to change you have to stop being afraid and get hold of yourself. Stop lying to yourself and making excuses. Get up, get out and start over. Just do it.

1. Do you feel you are your own hero? Why or why not?

___

2. What is the one goal you'd like to accomplish that you've been holding back on? Why have you been holding back?

___

3. What can you do to start to make your goal a reality?

___

Thank you.

I want to thank you for purchasing this workbook. I hope you've enjoyed completing it as much as I've enjoyed writing it and it helps you on your path toward your goal and your dream.

You can stay in touch with me at my website:
https://bjrichardsauthor.com

Or on my Facebook page:
https://www.facebook.com/BJ.Richards.Author/

And be sure to check out the other books I've written. You can see some of them on the Recommended Reading pages I've included here, or at my website.

Good luck on your journey to a happier, healthier you!

Recommended Reading

I'm sure you already have this, but if not, it's highly recommended you get a copy of the original work, as this workbook is a companion to it.

Girl, Wash Your Face: Stop Believing the Lies About Who You Are So You Can Become Who You Were meant to Be by Rachel Hollis

You may also be interested in some of my other books:

1) Find out what coconut oil can really do for you without all the hype. Check out my best-selling book: *Coconut Oil Breakthrough: Boost Your Brain, Burn the Fat, Build Your Hair* by BJ Richards

<u>Check it out here</u>: https://www.amazon.com/Coconut-Oil-Breakthrough-Boost-Brain-ebook/dp/B01EGBA1FW/

2) Do you have a dog? Here's another best seller you may be interested in. You'll find out to deal with a number of issues safely and inexpensively at home. Find out all about it in my best-seller: *Coconut Oil and My Dog: Natural Pet Health for My Canine Friend* by BJ Richards

<u>You can check it out here</u>: https://www.amazon.com/Coconut-Oil-My-Dog-Natural-ebook/dp/B01MUF93U1/

3) Did you know apple cider vinegar and baking soda have some amazing health benefits? Plus, you can use them for so many things in the home and save a ton of money.

You'll find out all about it my boxset: *Apple Cider Vinegar and Baking Soda 101 for Beginners Box Set* by BJ Richards

Check it out here: https://www.amazon.com/Apple-Cider-Vinegar-Baking-Beginners-ebook/dp/B07DPCLWGB/

You can also go **my website** to find even more books I've written and some recommended by other authors: https://bjrichardsauthor.com

www.ingramcontent.com/pod-product-compliance
Lightning Source LLC
Chambersburg PA
CBHW051353070526

44584CB00025B/3752